My Artbook

OrangeBooks Publication

1st Floor, Rajhans Arcade, Mall Road, Kohka, Bhilai, Chhattisgarh 490020

Website: **www.orangebooks.in**

First Edition, 2025

ISBN: 978-93-6554-915-7

My Artbook

- Rhea Gupta -

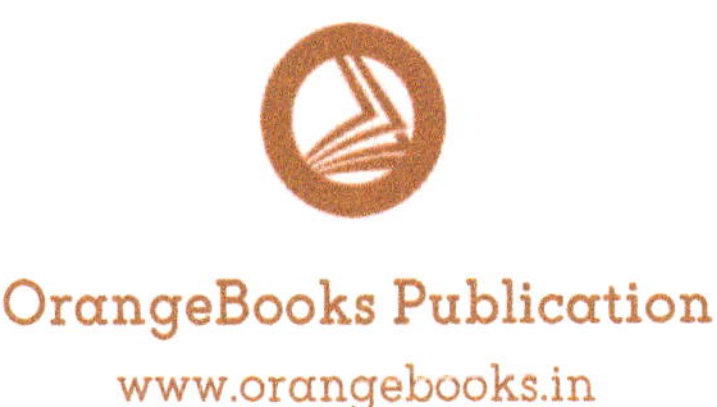

OrangeBooks Publication

www.orangebooks.in

Introduction

Paint pigments used in India are sourced from trees, shrubs, flowers and berries.

Like sandalwood, indigo, woad, madder, white chalk, limestone and many others;

To synthesis these paints many binder and gums are in the art of paint making like in old times from all around the globe.

Ingredients in paint making range from rainwater(distilled) to rabbit glue.

Other than paints, ink is made from pigments and binders.

Paints are generally in paste or liquid form while inks are especially of watery consistency.

There is an entire industry of paint and ink flourishing around the globe which is very inspiring for us artists.

Looking at a set of wonderful paint of acrylic or watercolour, no one can imagine what is going on in an artists's mind. From sketching to painting, every element of art is a masterpiece in itself.

Not only painting, there is art in chocolate making too to be telling the truth.

Today, the world in flowing with artists to the brim and to be one of them is so exciting.

I hope you enjoy looking at my examples of new art that I create everyday in my own art habitat at home.

Thanks for looking!

Rhea Gupta

Author

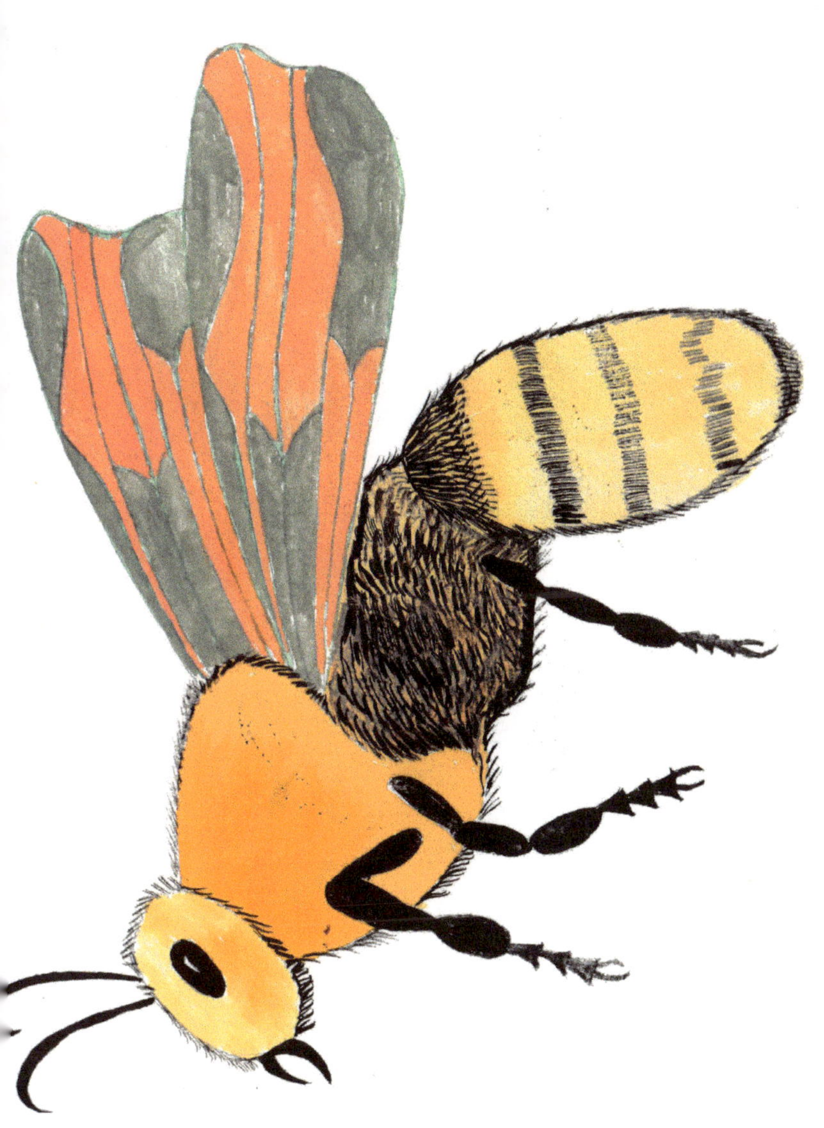

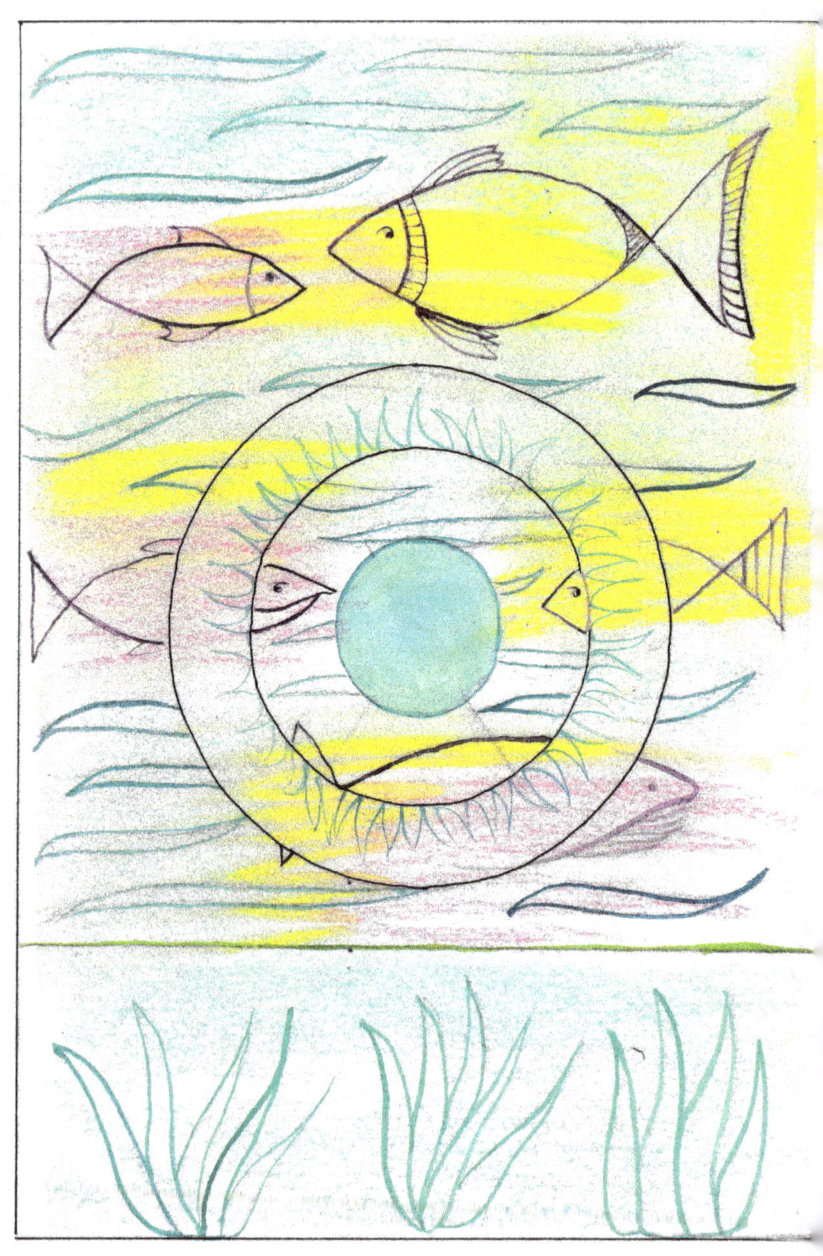

To ^knot do list.....

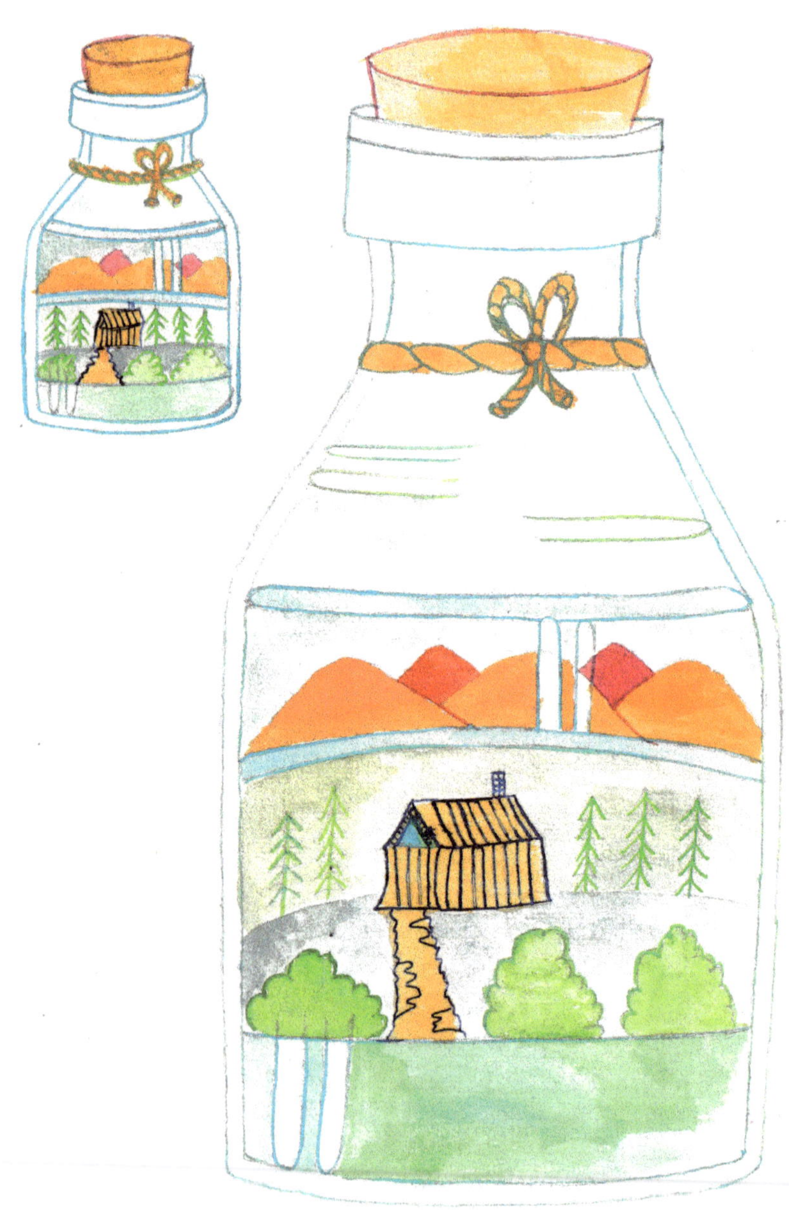

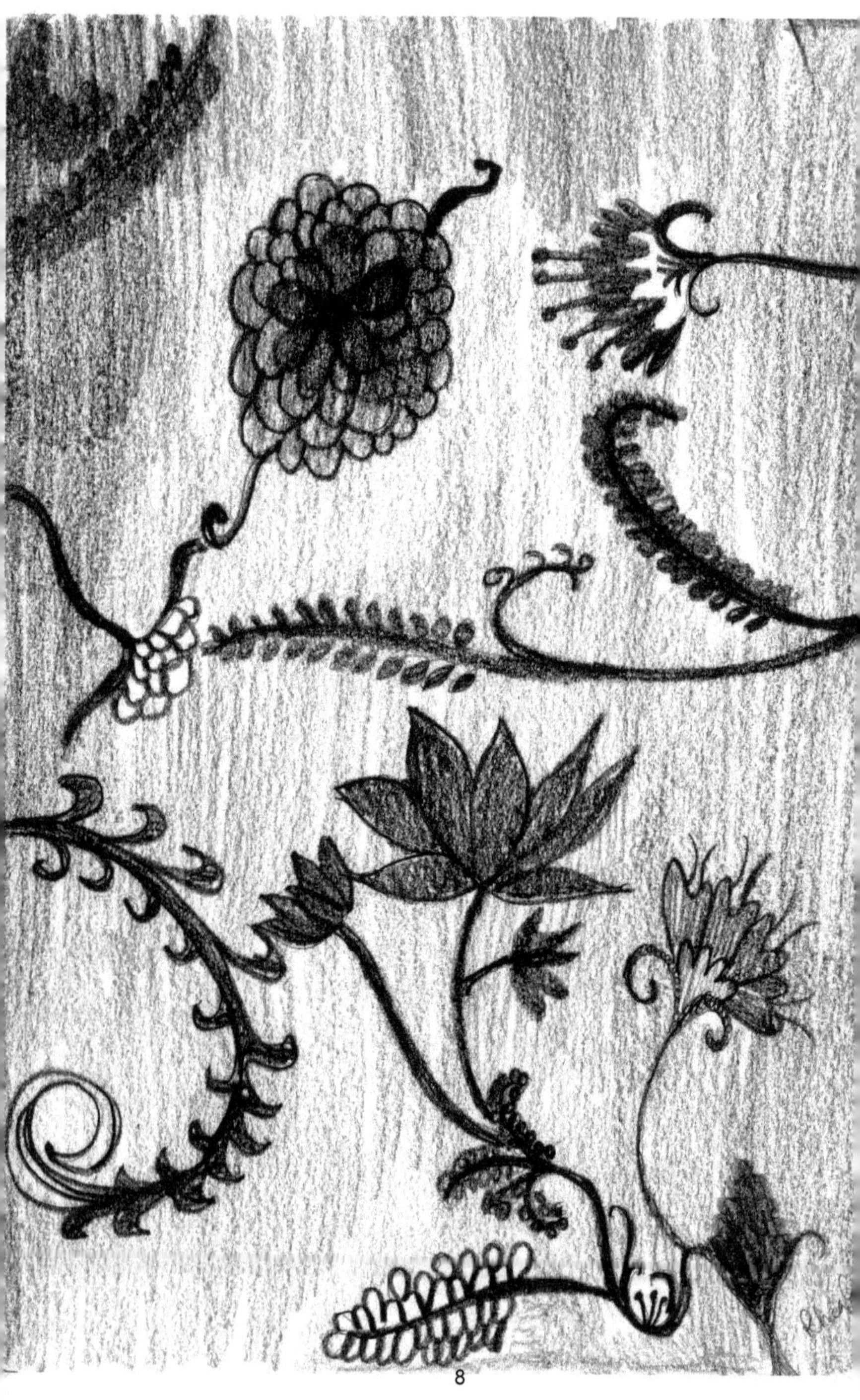

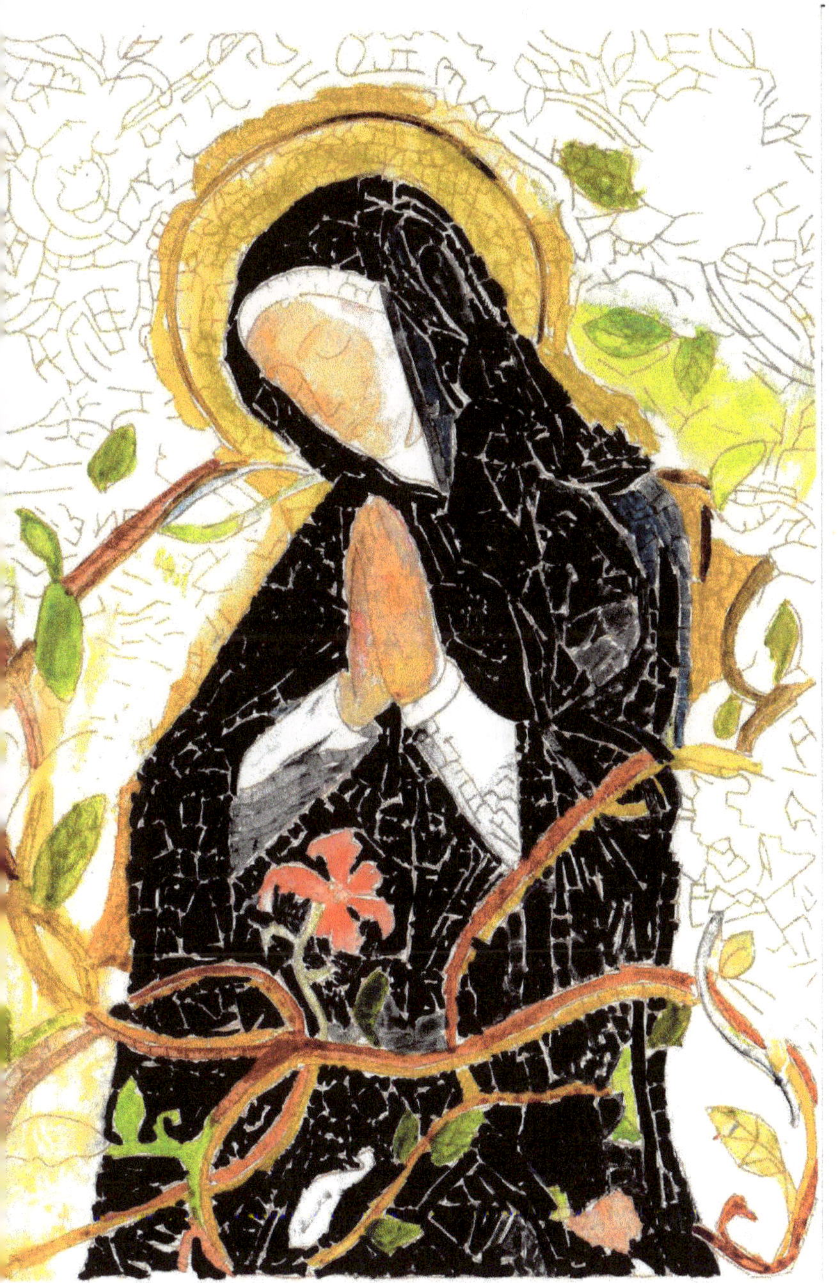

How a watch may be used as a Compass?

Point the hour hand to the sun. South is exactly half way between the hour hand and twelve on the watch. Counting forward upto noon but backward after the sun has passed the meridian.

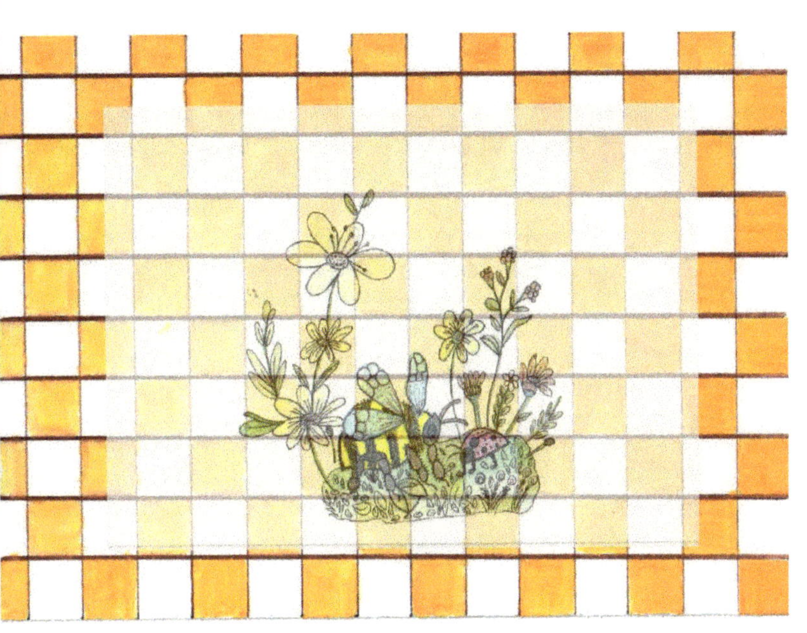

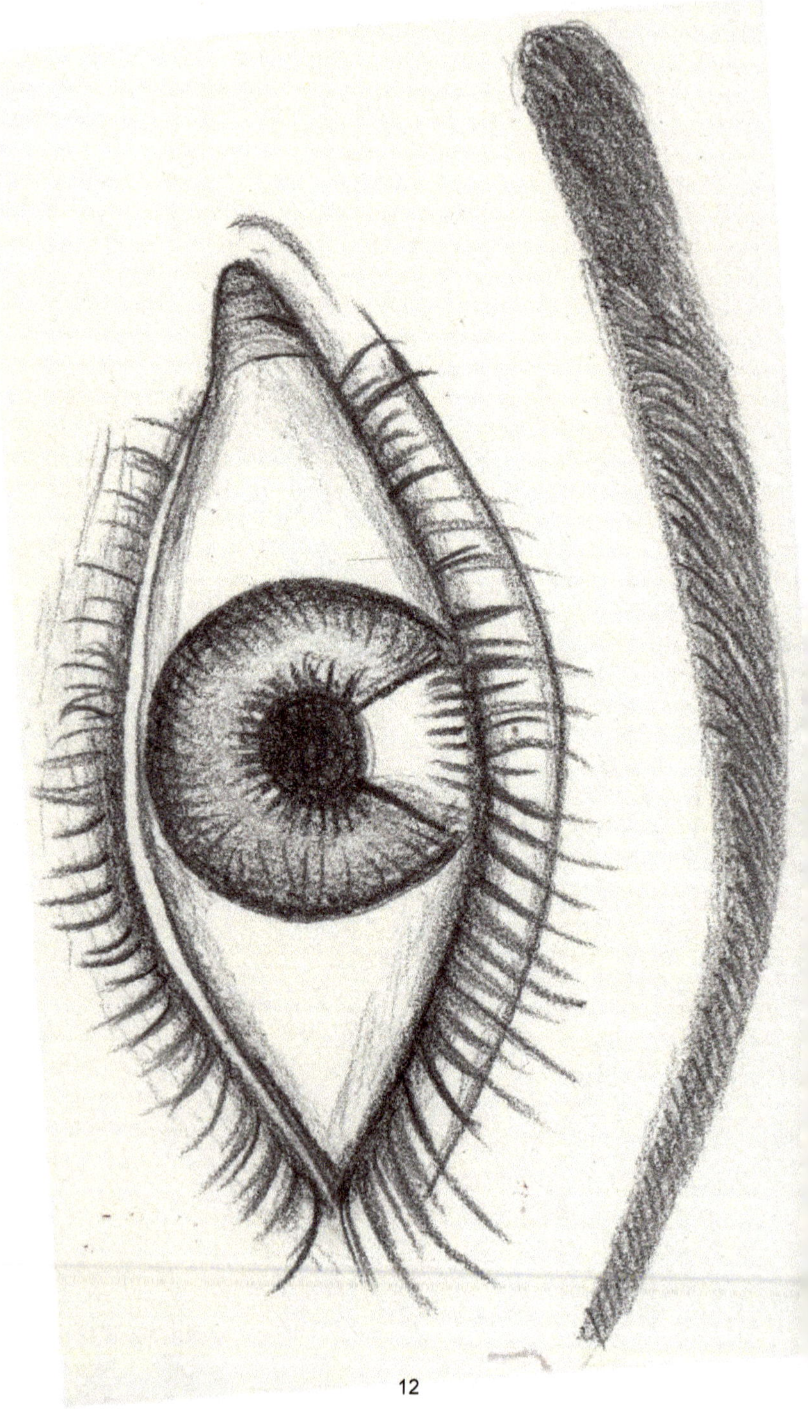

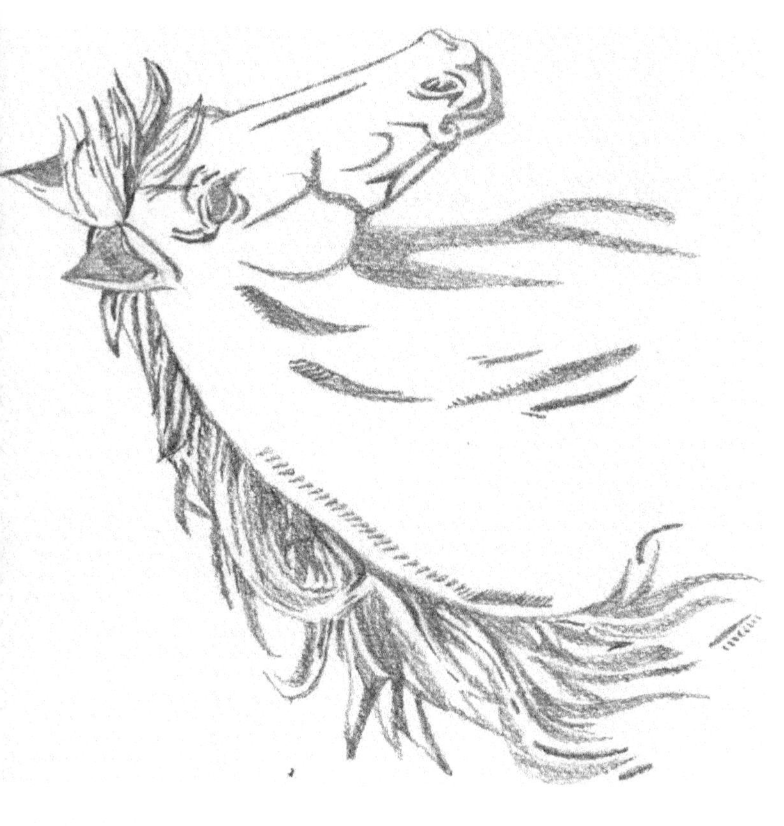

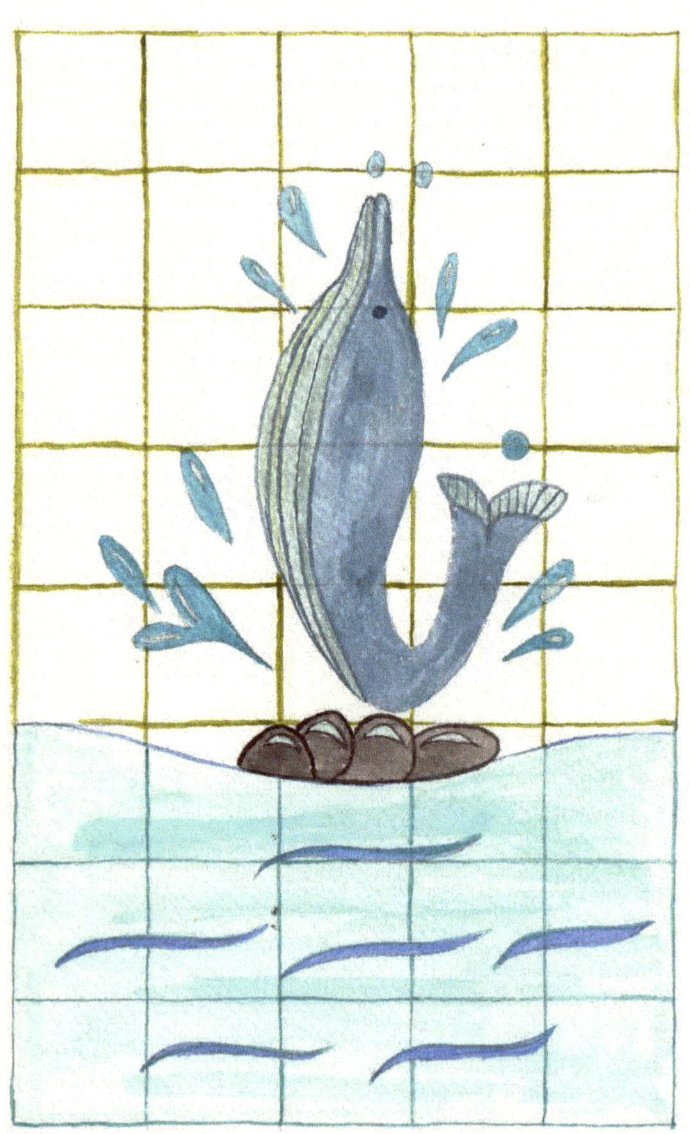

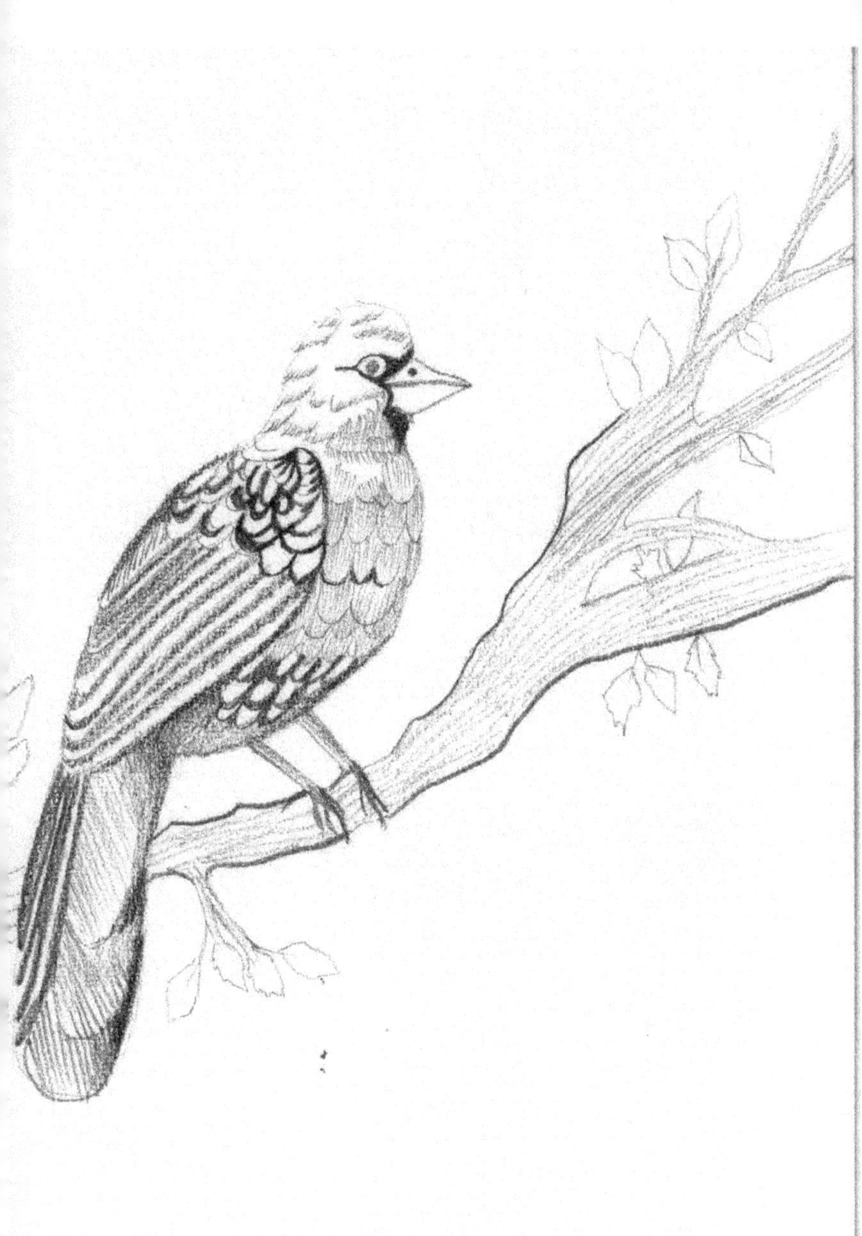

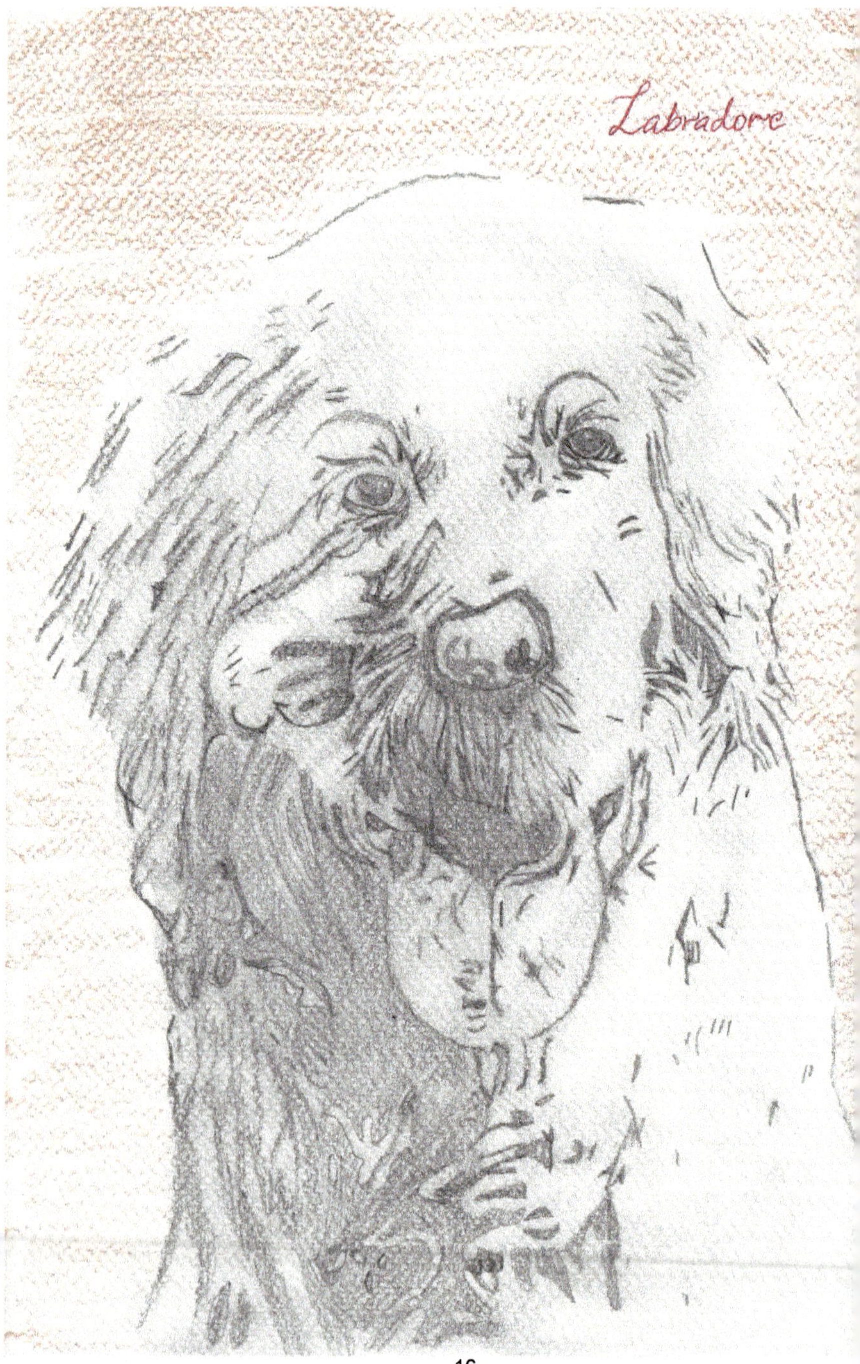
Labradore

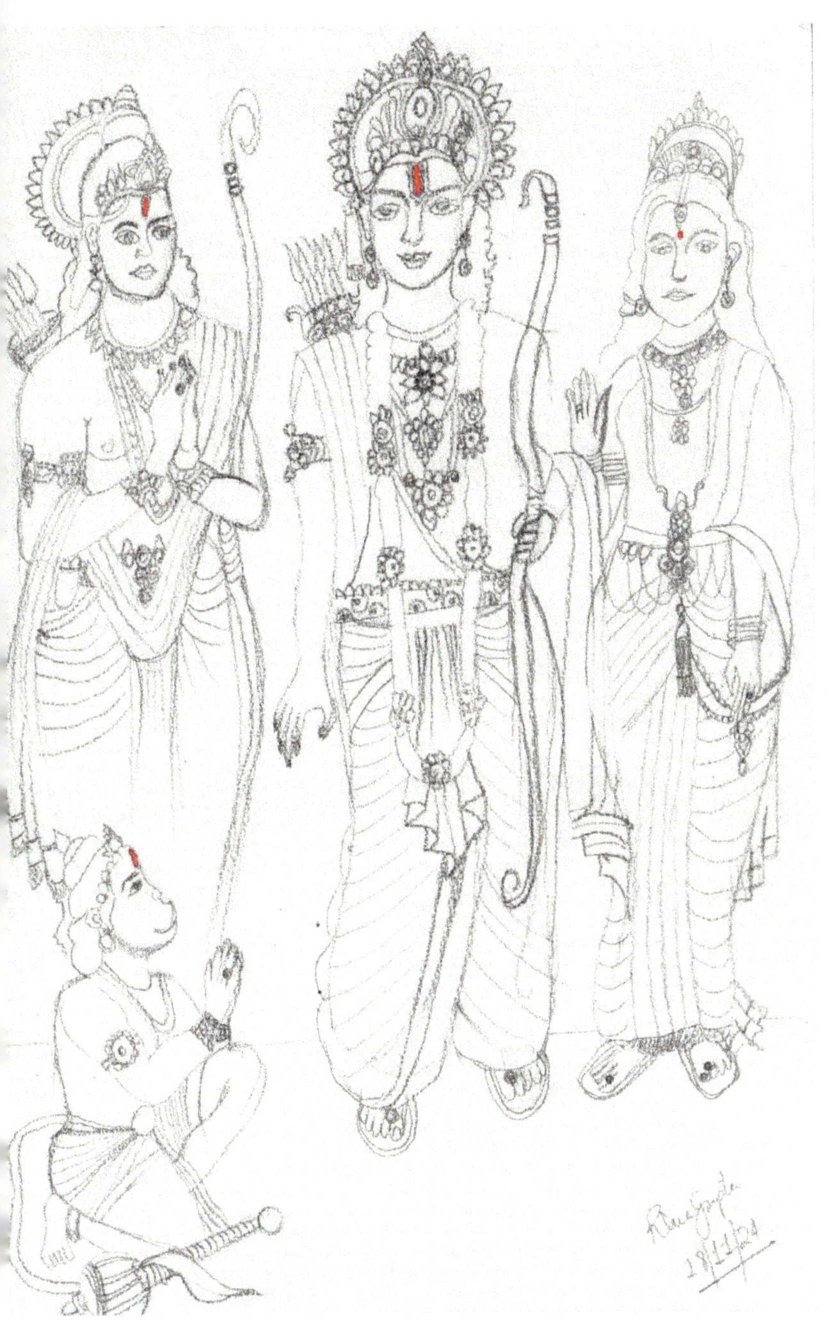

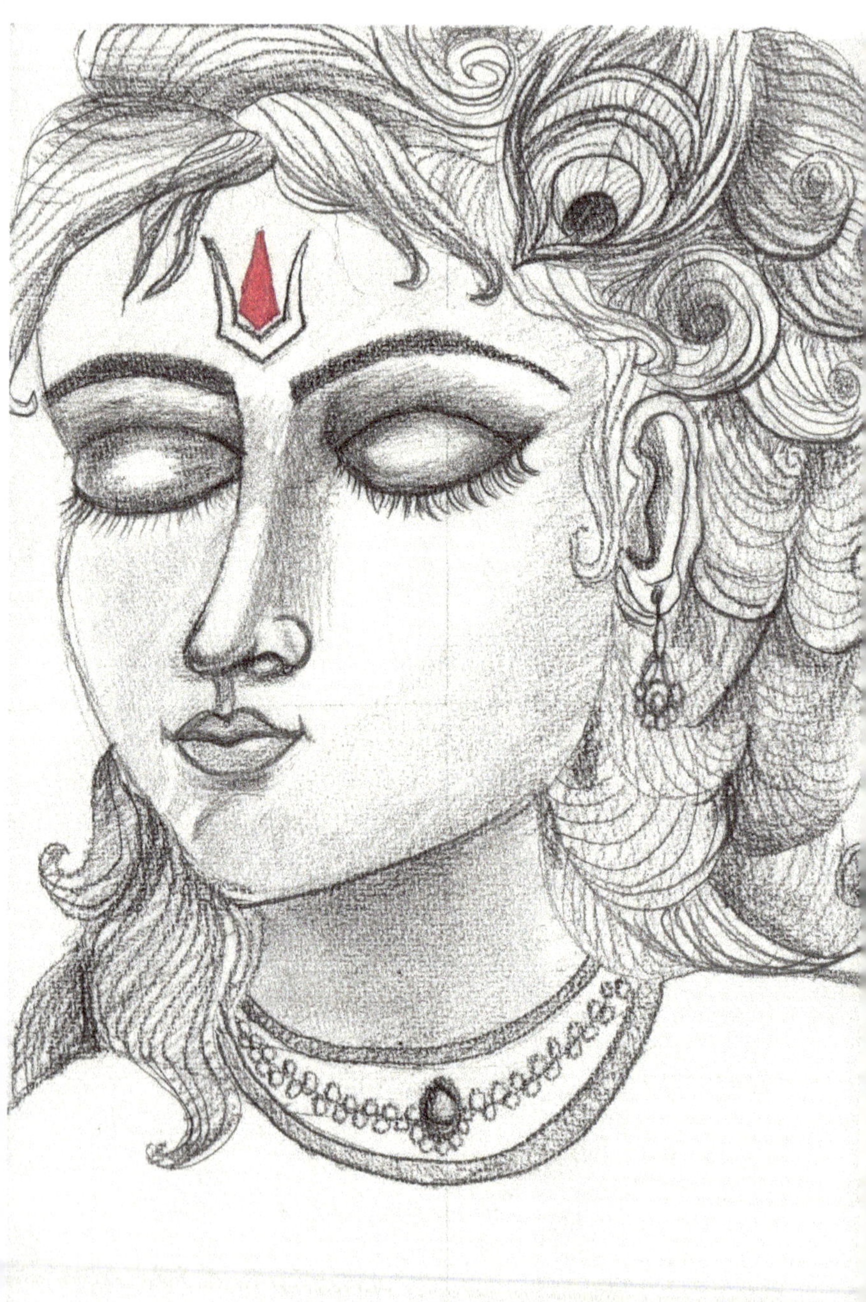

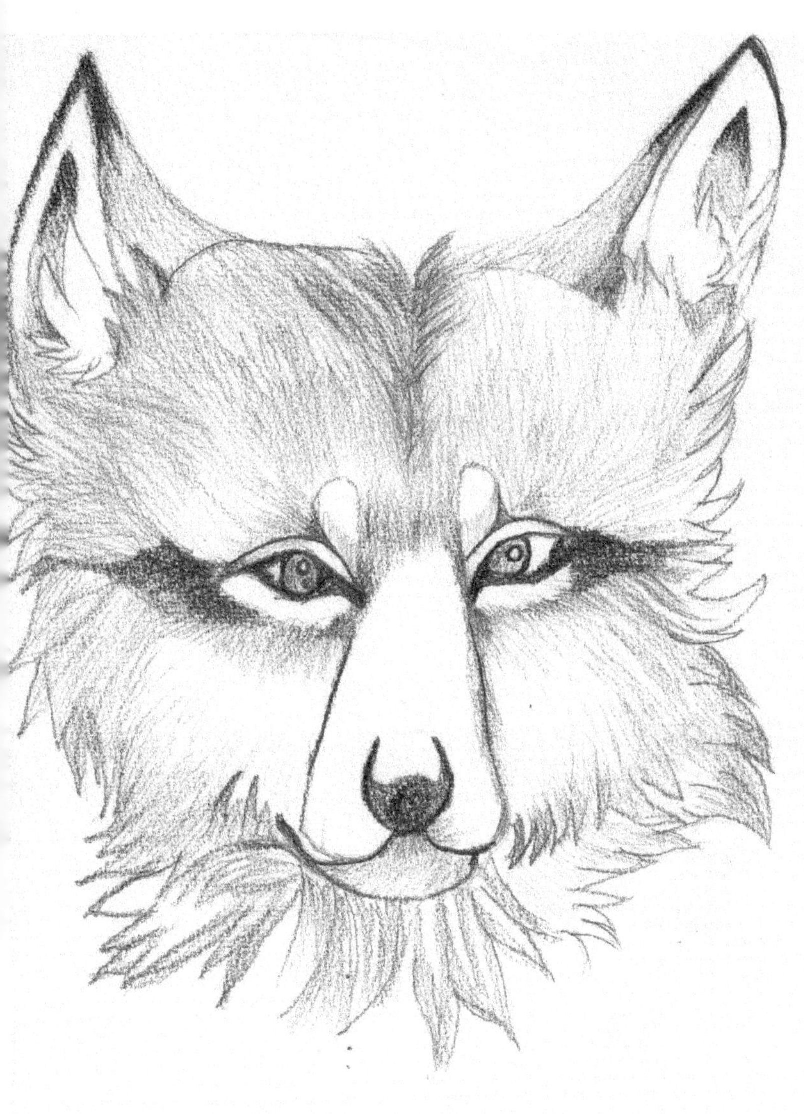

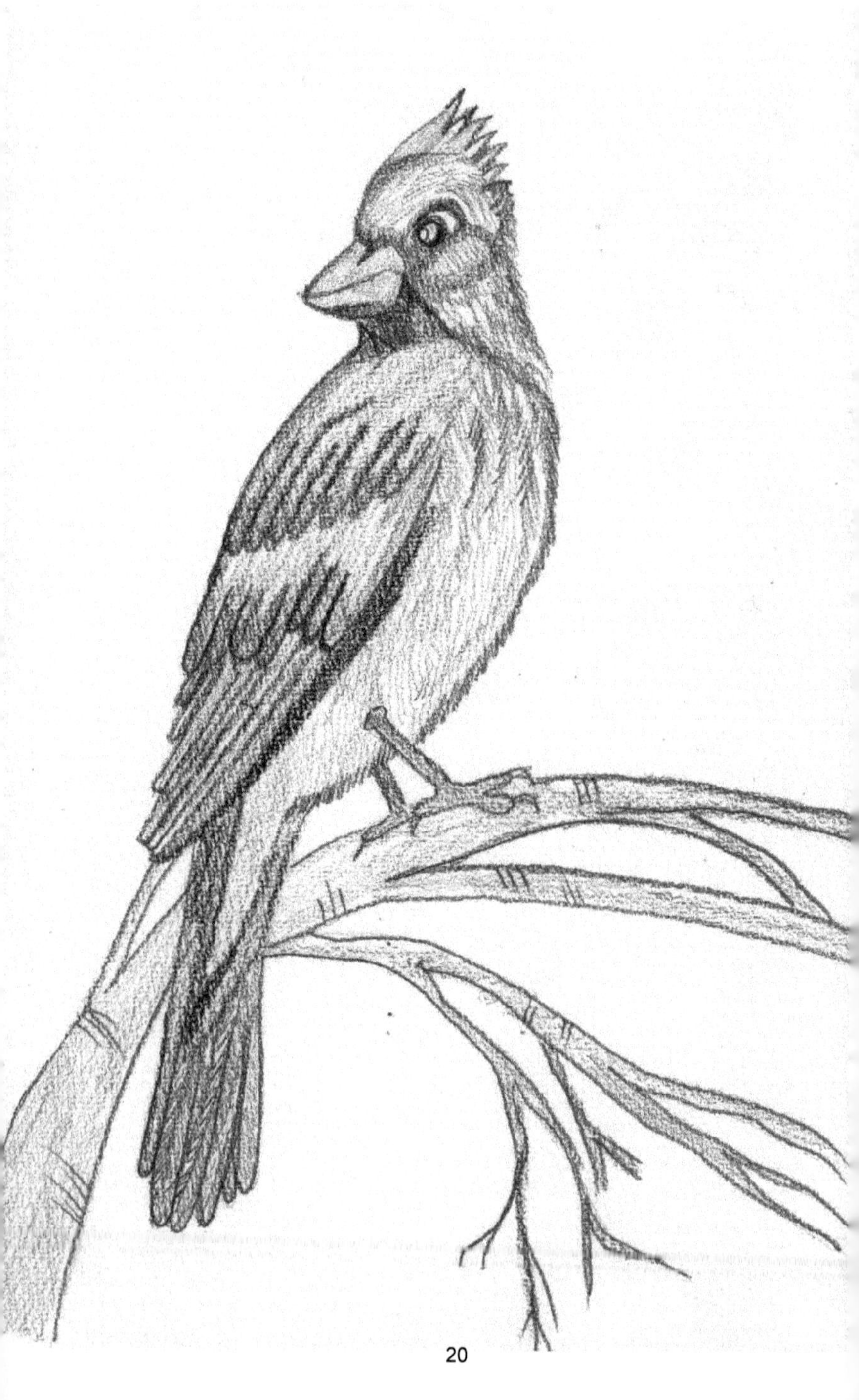

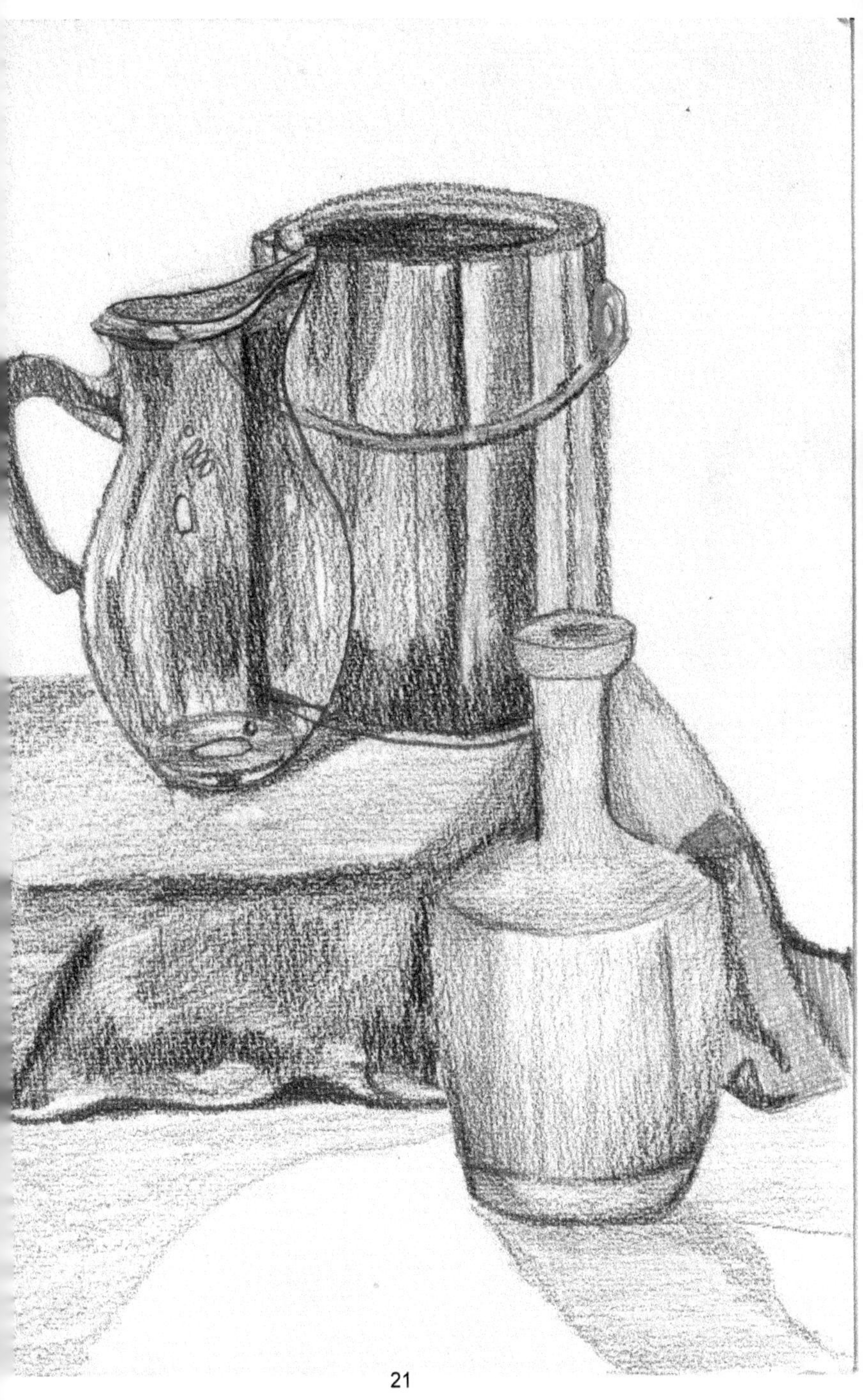

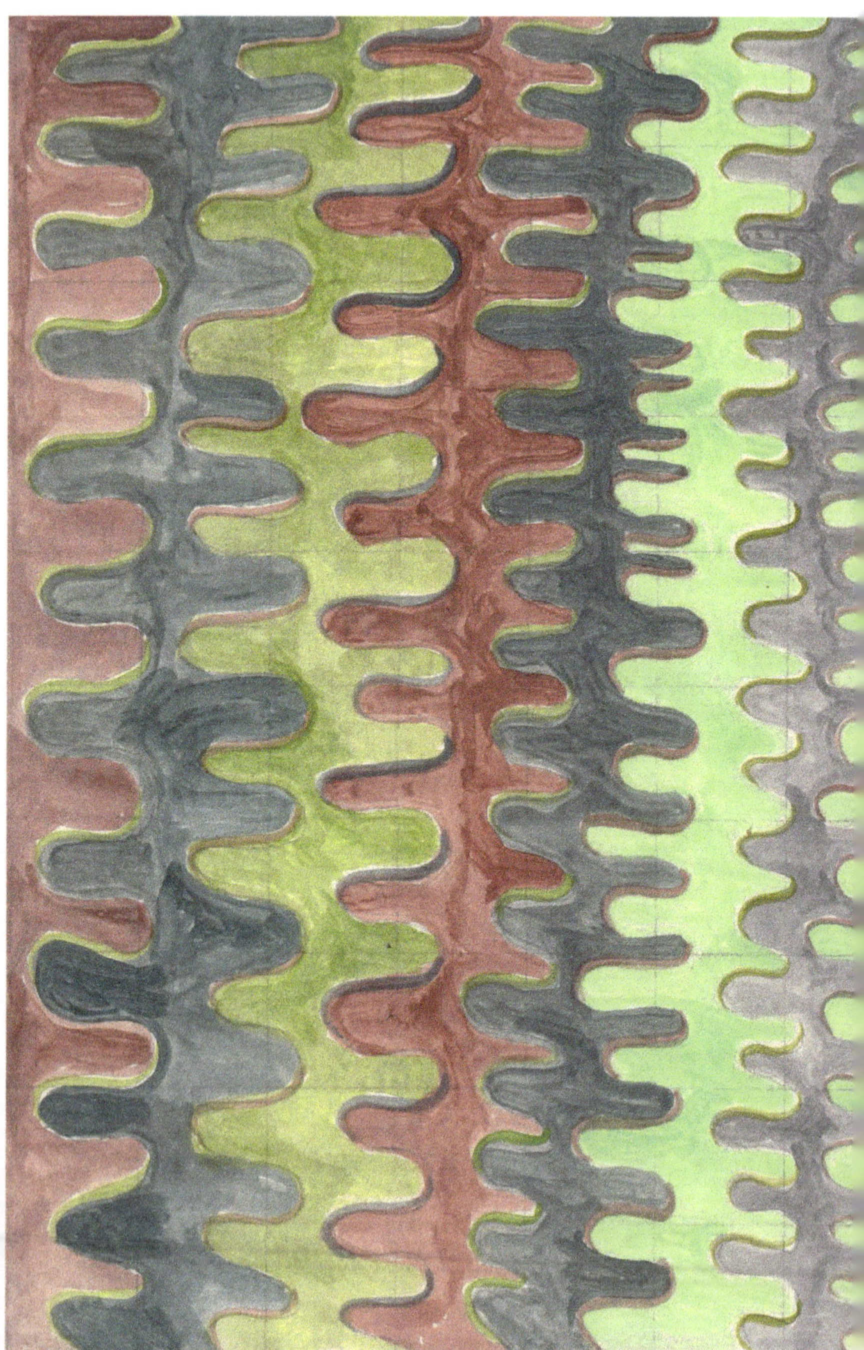

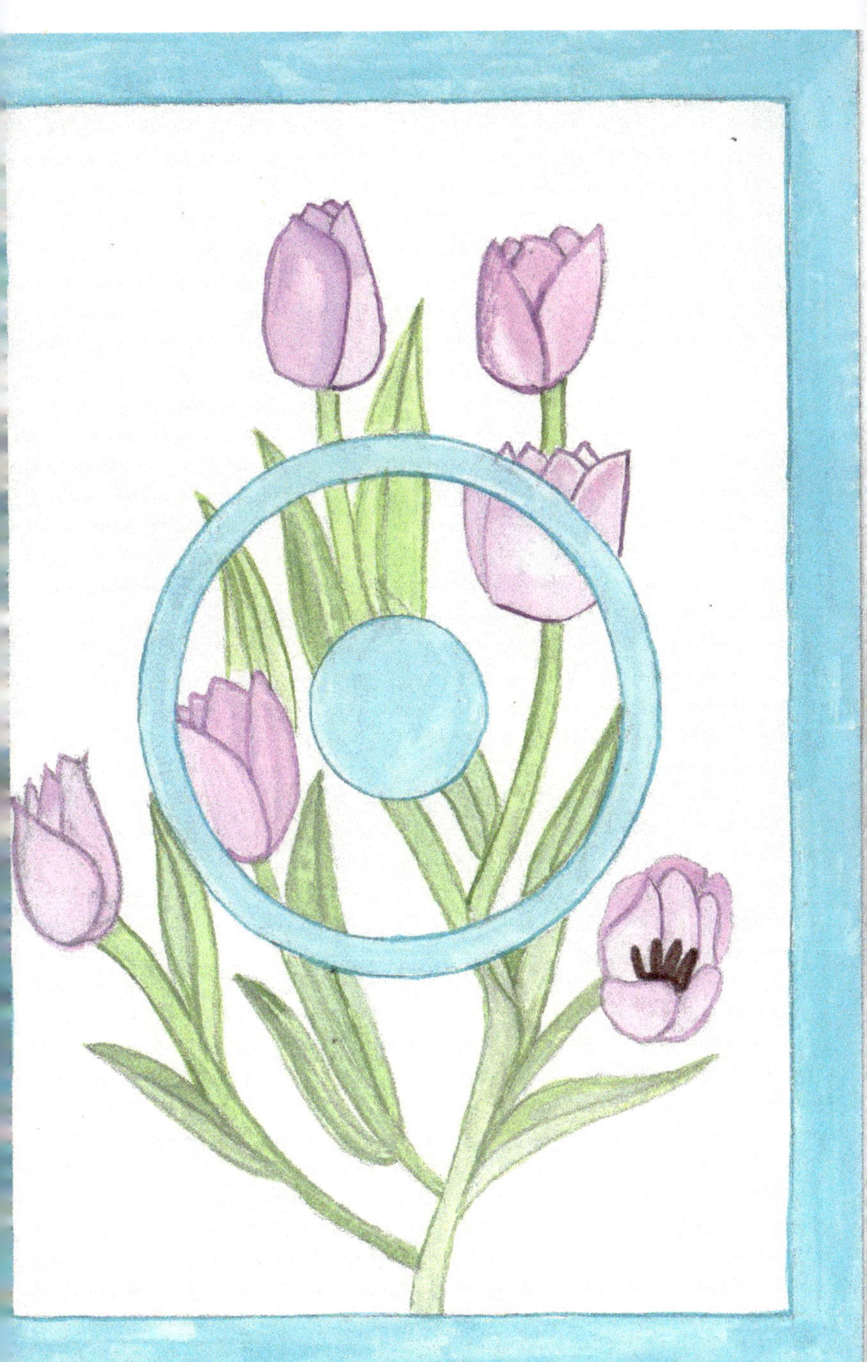

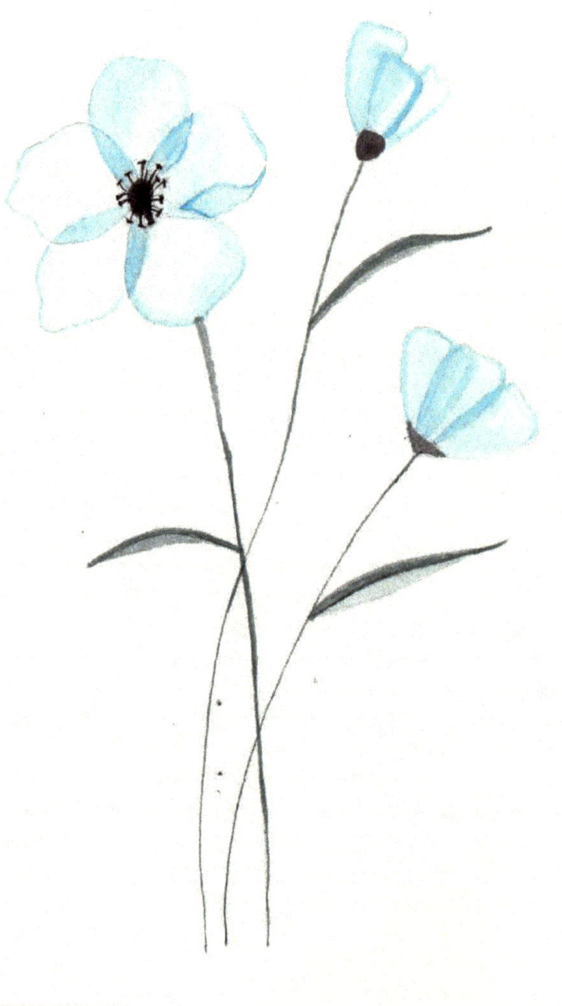

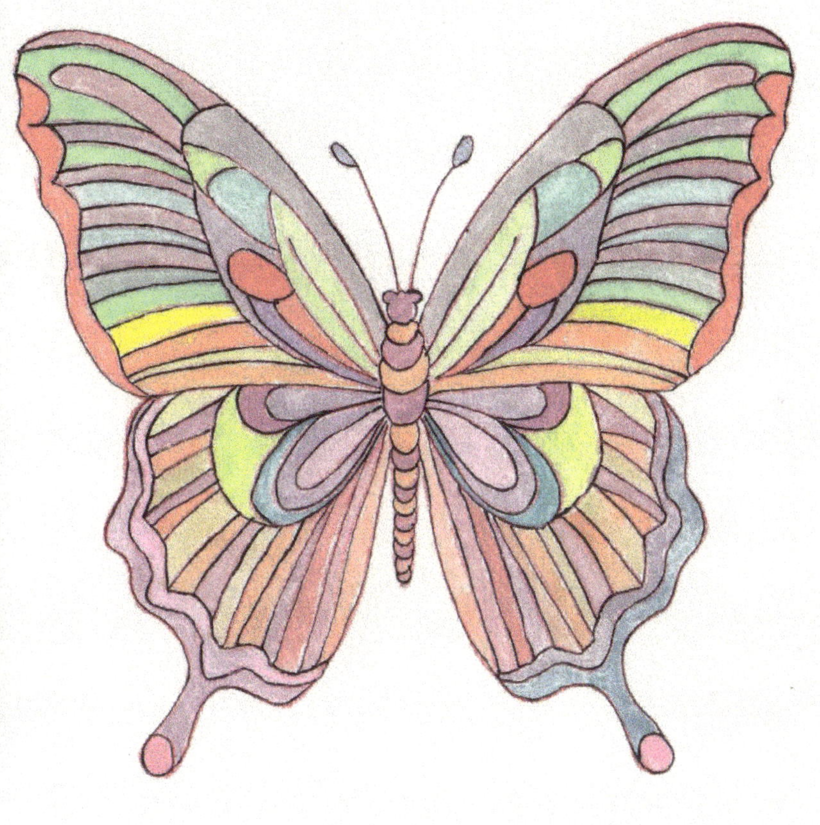

Butterfly

Rhea Gupta 25

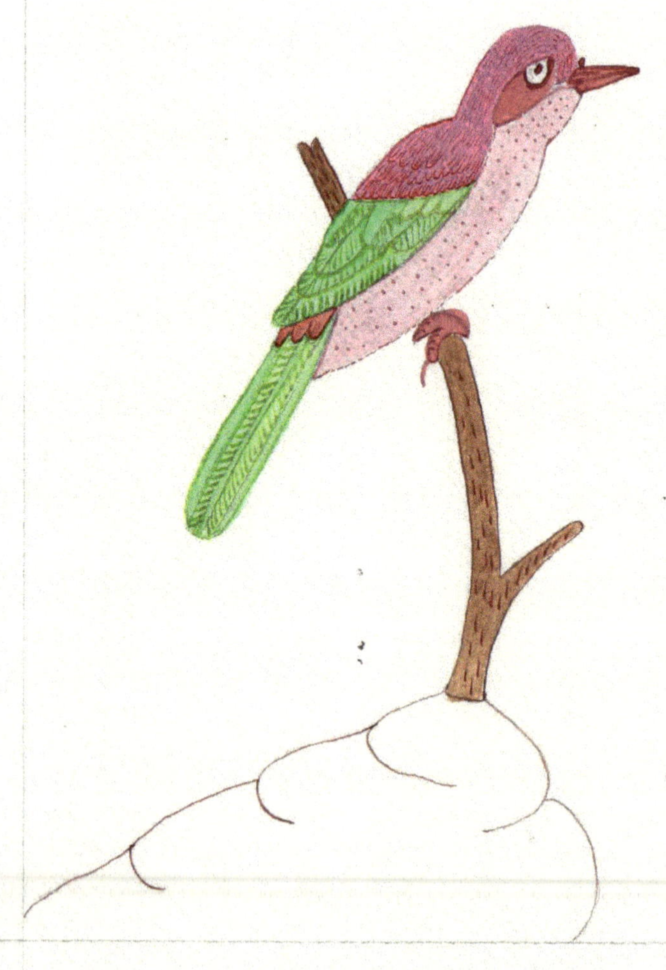

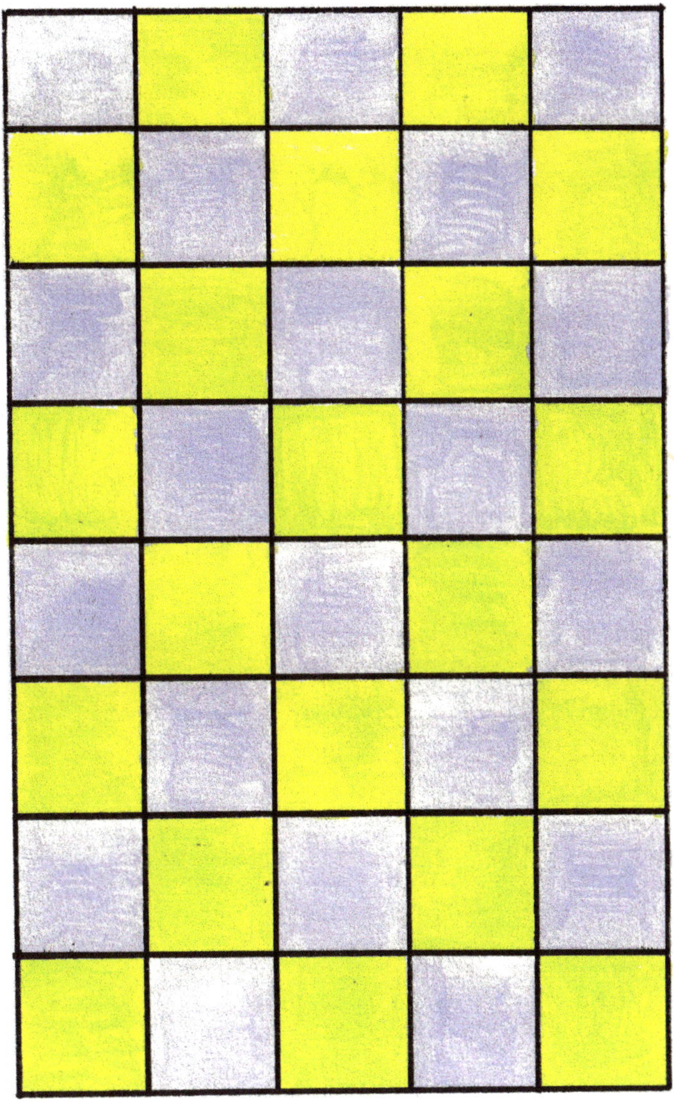

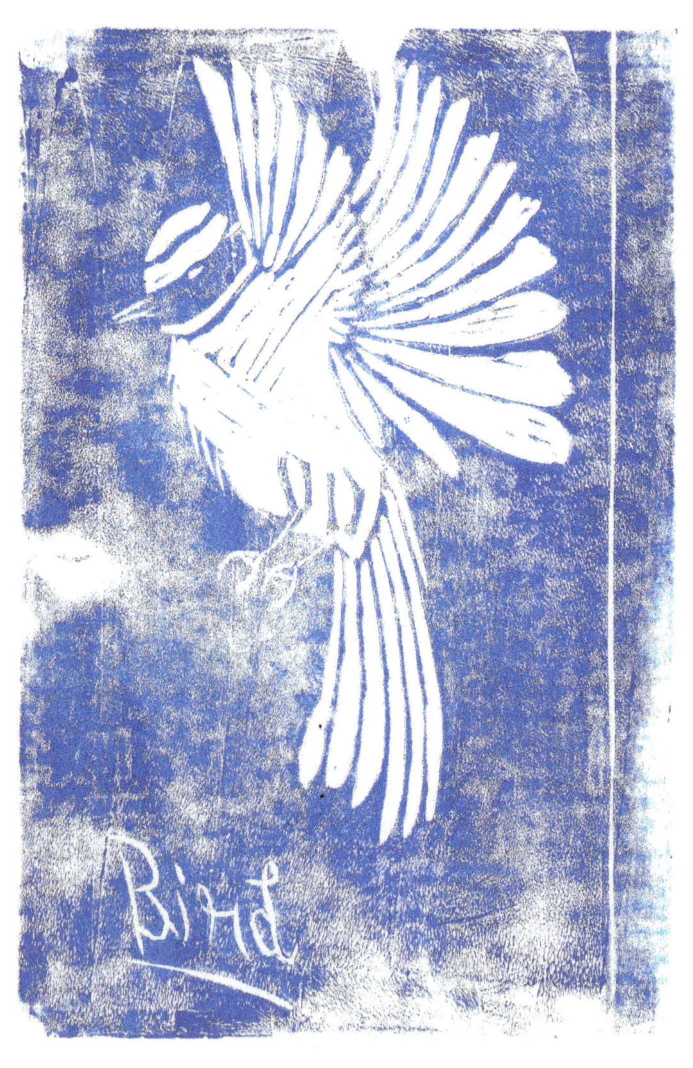

Bird

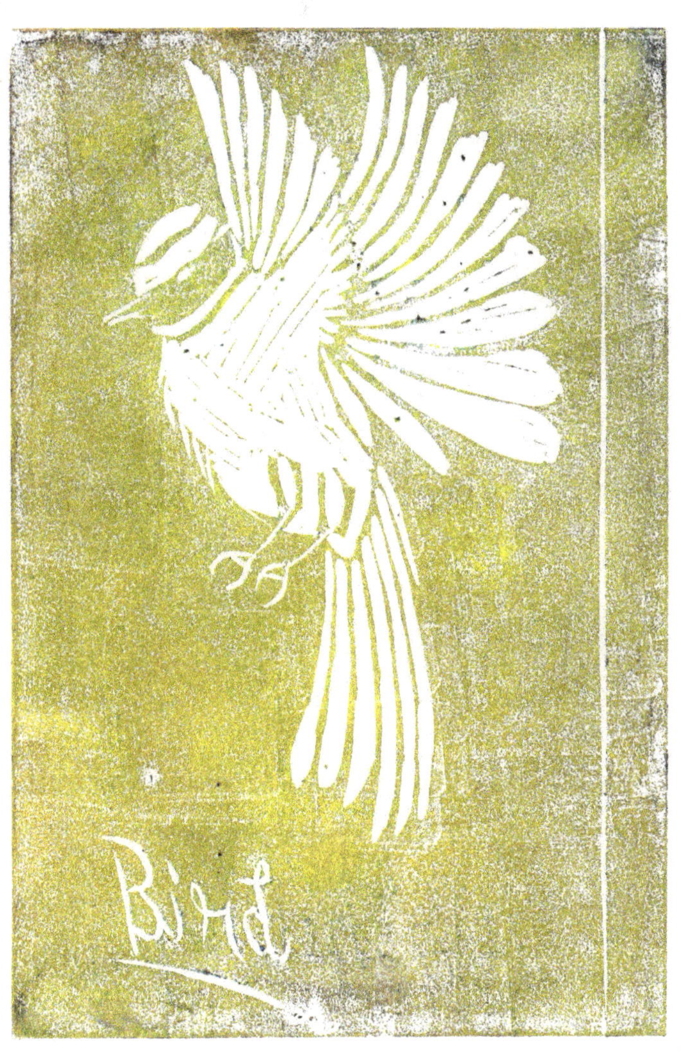

Bird

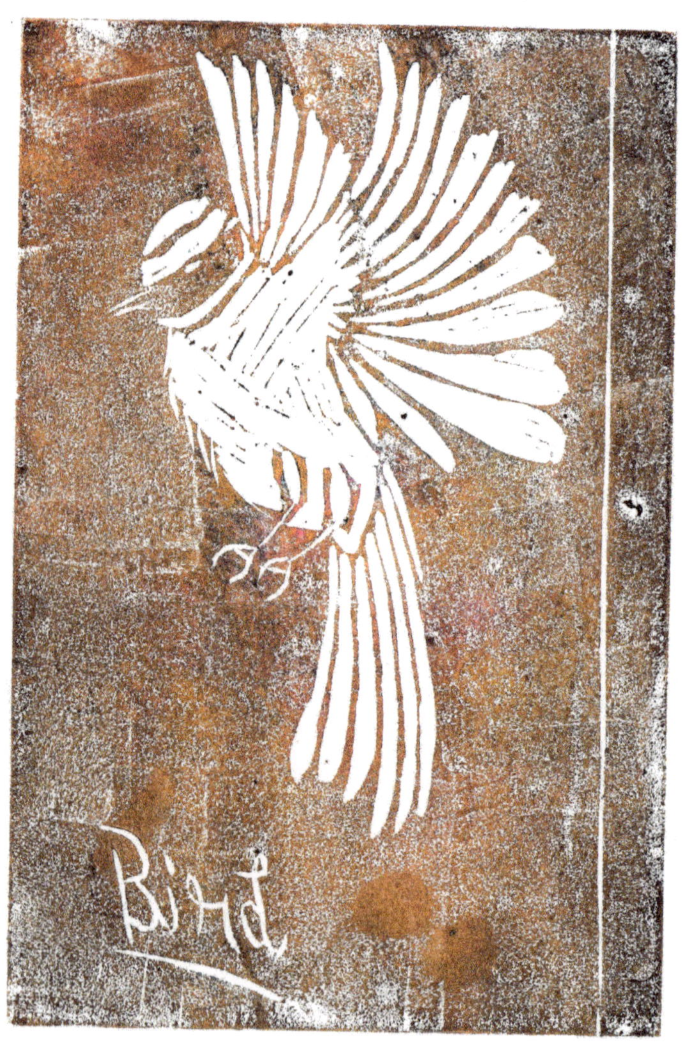

Bird

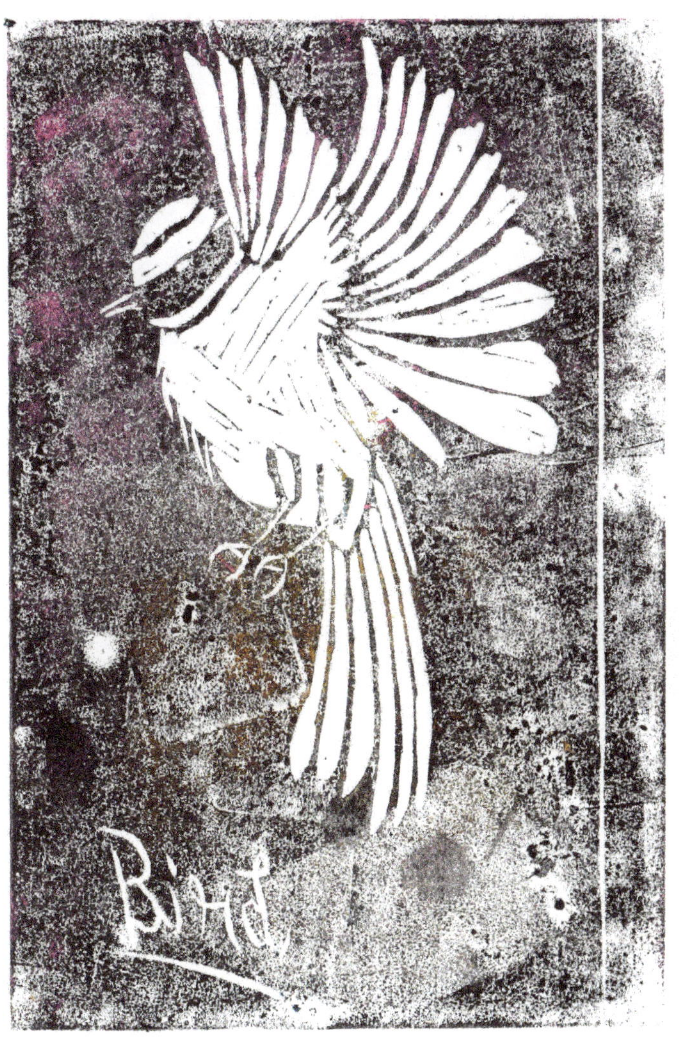

Bird

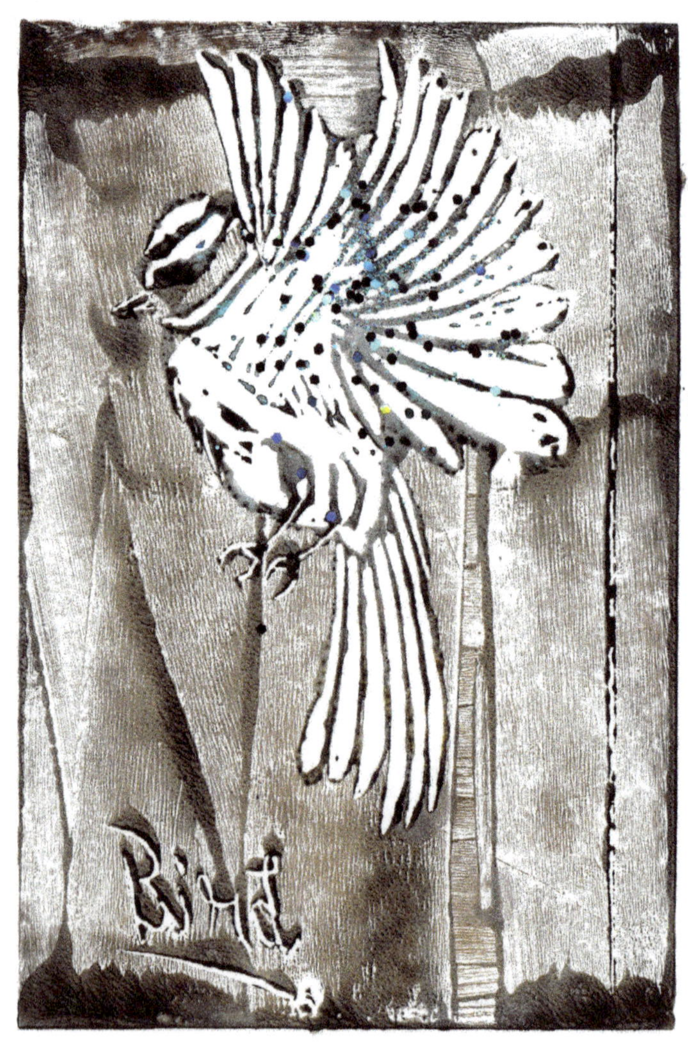